GERT

By the same author:

F-Words (2021)

Cavorting with Time (2018)

GERT

JACQUI MALINS

RECENT
WORK
PRESS
2015-2025
10 YEARS OF POETRY

Gert
Recent Work Press
Canberra, Australia

Copyright © Jacqui Malins, 2025

ISBN: 9781764106801 (paperback)

A catalogue record for this
book is available from the
National Library of Australia

All rights reserved. This book is copyright. Except for private study, research, criticism or reviews as permitted under the Copyright Act, no part of this book may be reproduced, stored in a retrieval system, or transmitted in any form by any means without prior written permission. Enquiries should be addressed to the publisher.

Cover and internal images by Jacqui Malins (see List of illustrations, p. 147)
Cover design: Jacqui Malins and Recent Work Press
Set by Recent Work Press

recentworkpress.com
10 YEARS OF POETRY

This is a work of documented history, oral history, and imagination.

The endnotes indicate which is which.

Contents

Prologue	3
Formation	9
Girl	33
Mother	59
Matriarch	91
Thereafter	119
Epilogue	137
Acknowledgements	142
Endnotes	143

Map of Tasmania and Queenstown:
Graphic by author. References: Map of Tasmania is from D. W. Lewin's *The Eucalypti, Hardwood Timbers of Tasmania,* Gray Brothers, Hobart, 1906; and folded map from 'A Guide to Tasmania, the Premier Health Resort of the Commonwealth', Tasmanian Government Railways Dept, Hobart, 1906.

TASMANIA.

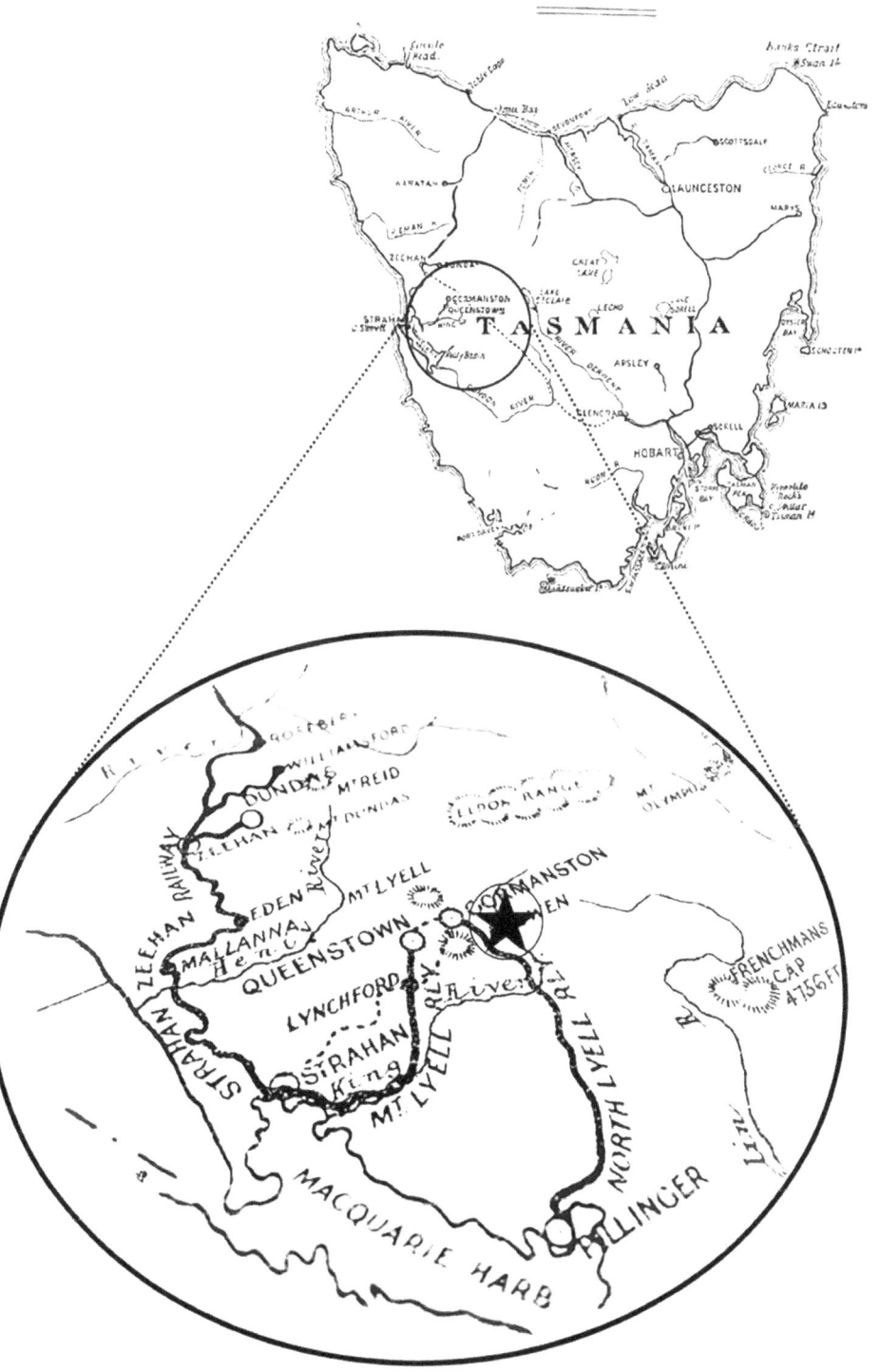

PROLOGUE

PHOTO TAKEN 1924. KNOWN AS THE 18 MILE ABOUT THE GOVERNOR RIVER ON THE NORTH MOUNT LYELL RAILWAY BETWEEN CROTTY & KELLY BASIN. (GERT BROWN EIGHTEEN YEARS OF AGE.) JUST HAD HER CURLY HAIR CUT OFF BEFORE THIS PHOTO WAS TAKEN. TED STREET WITH BLACK COCKATOO ON DOUBLE BARREL GUN. THEY WILL NO WHAT THE COCKATOO IS ABOUT IF THEY GRAB HOLD OF HIM. BY: FINGER.

Photograph of Gert Brown and Ted Street (photographer unknown) with typewritten caption by Eric Thomas. Reproduced with permission from the Queenstown Galley Museum.

In the Galley Museum, Queenstown, Tasmania, 2018

A wall of framed photographs.
One of many walls
in many rooms.

Typewritten captions
ALL CAPS capture
Eric Thomas' cache
of local knowledge.

Your face, Gert, through glass.
Pale curl-capped oval
glows behind
(within)
my spectral reflection.

You squint a little in the sun
and—grin? I lean in.
Your expression
is harder to discern.

T-strap shoes, white stockings
striped by buttongrass.
Gauzy mountain flutters
behind your head

Each hand grasps the tail
of a splayed black cockatoo.
The young man beside you
holds his gun point-blank.

No—a parallax illusion.
A third bird sits up on
its double-barrelled perch,
points a bright eye at the camera.

Your human companion's gaze
turns askance.

Like the bird
you look back.

The Princess River

i have had other names in other tongues
      but it is so long since anyone spoke them in my hearing
          i have forgotten the sounds

              perhaps someone will remind me one day
                things are being forgotten
                  and remembered
                    all the time

          i talk to the queen and king
        to my minor tributary siblings
      at our confluences we whisper

flowing lapping trickling rippling seeping
    flowing lapping trickling rippling seeping
        flowing lapping trickling rippling seeping

            i talk to the sky too, the clouds, rain, mist and moon
                to the rocks and earth that hold me
                    to the chipped stones and glassy blades
                        bricks, timbers, broken bottles
                            and pottery i have swallowed.

                    flowing lapping trickling rippling seeping
                    flowing lapping trickling rippling, seeping

                i eavesdrop on the people who come near
              though these days they aren't many
                      or often
            i have heard geologists talk
          a mouthful of river stones
        conglomerate dolerite orogeny
      i have heard people murmur
     like the breeze ripples my surface
    shout like my roar in flood
   listened to children chatter
pebbles in a riffle.

flowing lapping trickling rippling seeping

      i will tell you what i have seen
            heard
                know

Acknowledgement

I acknowledge
the Palawa people of Lutruwita
the Lairmerenga of the West Coast hinterland.
I pay respect
to the Elders, past and present
to the Old People whose presence I have felt
to the young people
who are learning, telling and living the stories
the knowledge
suppressed ignored submerged
for far too long

FORMATION

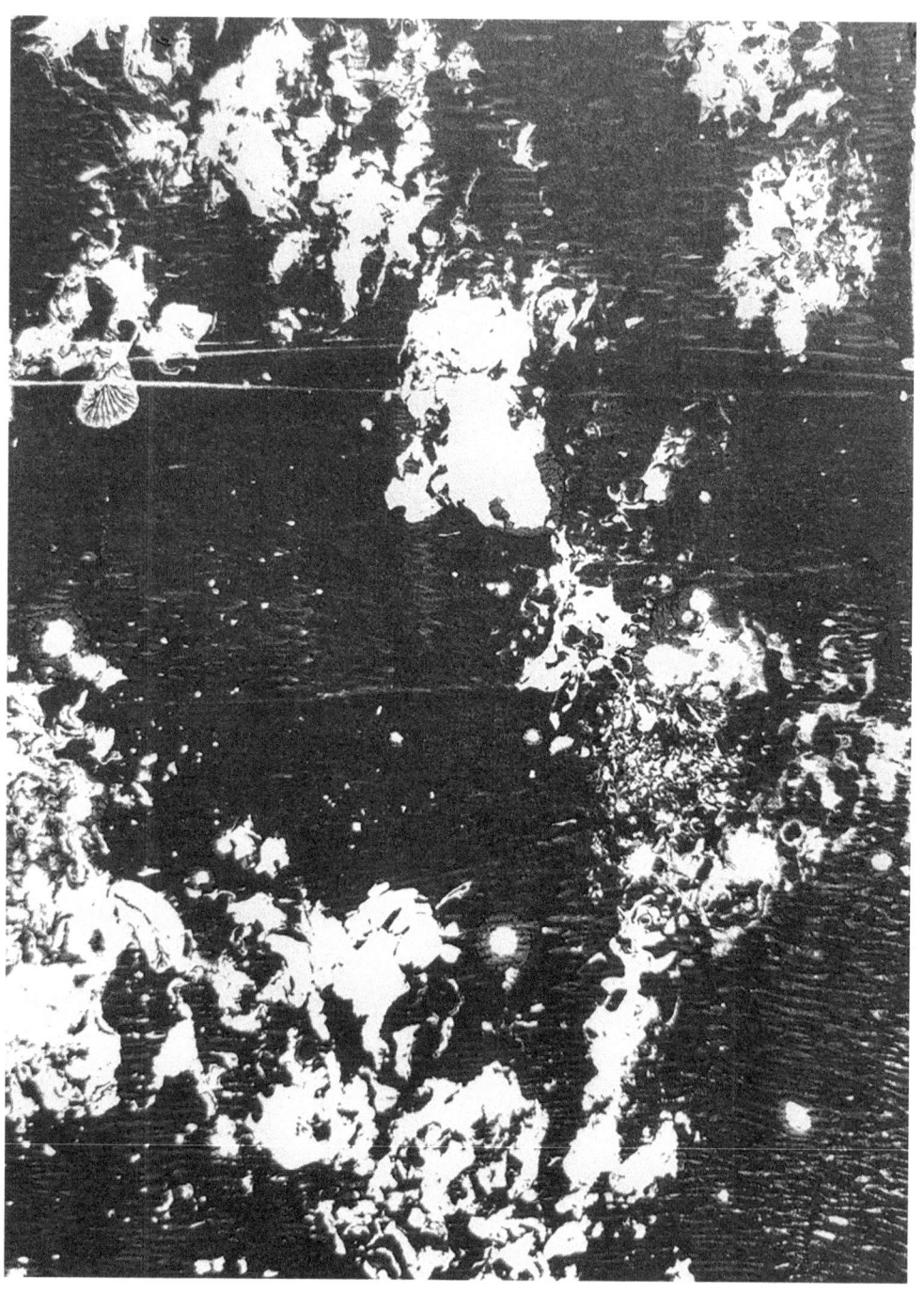

Terrain

        a sphere congeals
       in space—hot cold hot
     a slow sweating of seas
    the scabbing up of land

  nuna rodinia gondwana
 glide over molten foundations
variations of landmass
 forming and reforming

   the panthalassa laps at pangaea
    reefs accrete—drown—are buried
      magmas ooze between the earth's fascia
       harden into lustrous veins
        of gem and metal
            crystallise into pillars that crumble
              roll into boulders and stones
                  are obliterated into dust

                       flash
                      impact
                    heatandlight

                 earth vaporises
                fuses green glass

          greedy ice
        eats the ocean
      groans
      grates
     remakes this
      terrain

Discovery

people come
   curious explorers of new country
      walk across the bassian plain
         and up the ranges

            electric sky
               waves veils of colour
                  across the stars

                     the explorers find rivers
                        valleys grasslands tundra
                           ice cap slick over plateau
                         bounteous water

                            the explorers stay
                           learn this place
                           eat and drink of it
                         become its intimates
                       beget new generations
                     remember their journey
                 in story

               hunt wallaby, wombat
               find dry hospitable caves
               dolerite and rock crystal for sharp tools
               a greenish glass for the finest blades

                       ice is melting
                         retreating up valleys
                             cataracts cut canyons
                             trees advance
                               ferns thicken
                                   cool fire won't keep
                                     the rainforest at bay
                                       wallaby and wombat
                                           vanish
                                           with the
                                              grass

Cut off

sea strangles peninsula into
island. plain becomes strait
severs these peoples
from all others for
ten thousand
years.

Lairmerenga

The King River lies
on the lands of the Lairmerenga.
Links plateau to coast.
Travelling country.
Gathering country.

Land of good fishing
and grass tree bread.
Spirits fed by rich history
hidden in ancient caves.

In spring, people from south and east
follow the path markers
carved by their ancestors.
Meet the Lairmerenga
And travel north together
to gather mutton bird eggs.

For marriage, the clans gather.
Consecrate the corroboree grounds
with song and dance.

In summer the Lairmerenga
exchange ancient courtesies
and gifts for safe passage.

Travel east to feast on the gifts of the sea
and dance with the coastal peoples.
To trade bark string and baskets.
Rare ochre for ceremony.
Go north again
for the grown mutton birds.

The sick and old wait, welcome
on Lairmerenga country
until their people's return.

At death, cremation.
The spirits left alone
to reclaim the dead.
Ashes and bone
taken away by
winter rains.

Huon pine

tendrils of yellow smoke
    curl out from scaly branchlets.

        the smoulder of life

           pollen grains like mist
           bathe one tree after another
           dust my surface gold

    flowing lapping trickling rippling seeping
    flowing lapping trickling rippling seeping

  cones swell fecund
drop seed
 onto ground
  embellished
    with lichen and fungi
      rocks napped with moss

        seeds sprout
           push roots down
              shoots up
                  build slender concentric rings
                  around golden hearts

                    in my stream
                      this tree's centuries-old ancestors
                        lie whole and fresh
                          steeped in their own oil
                            incorruptible as holy relics

                      they remember gold

                    i run over and around them
              flowing lapping trickling rippling seeping

            in this tree's future
            there is fire and axe

              this tree's future
                in two thousand years.

Arrivals

New people come. Land cautiously
gratefully, having traversed many seas.

At first they cling to the shore
build fortresses of wood and stone.

Emboldened, send out tendrils of track.
Cut, burn, hack, dig, map.

Country pushes back, but they thrust on
through what they call 'wilderness'.

James Erskine Calder breaks his way
past Frenchman's Cap. Finds bark huts

shaped like beehives. Empty, but only lately.
One is painted: a man spears a kangaroo

there is a wild dog, an emu. Calder
names the place *the painted plain.*

Doesn't wait to see if the artist returns.
To learn who they are. Where they go.

Naming and taming

                                              they see
                                       extraordinary paucity
                             anything but agreeable
                       somewhat displeasing
             a disagreeable monotony
       void of animation
   scenes of utter lifelessness
desolation

  they see we rivers run fast
    and always away
       flowing lapping trickling rippling seeping
          they try to bring us into empire
              name us king queen princess governor
                 invest the peaks above
                    with their kind of enlightenment
                        call them darwin owen sedgewick jukes lyell

                        on some days
                      even they can see
                       the serried outline
                           of these beautiful mountains
                             magnificent myrtle forest
                           are moved to name
                           a lower hill
                           or lesser tributary
                           The Bird
                           The Fish

Disappearances I

Between characters and lines
I search
the archive.

Disappearances move among
the forest of letters
cloaked in possum fur or darkness
blend into the punctuation
by craft or design.

Are written
into scripts
and histories.
to appear as natural
as officially believed

Crucible

Prospectors, investors and speculators
want to know what is below.
They have high hopes.

Metallurgists perform assays
heat samples to white-gold glow.

1859: Gould finds lead
traces of copper and gold.

1881: Lynch strikes gold
and miners swarm the valley.

1883: The McDonough brothers and Karlson
believe the Iron Blow hides gold.
Indebted, disappointed, they sell their claim
to Henry, Dixon and Crotty.

Days later their buyers
strike the payload.

1885: Glover finds iron ore, nearly pure.

1891: Viable copper is dug
by Crotty, Kelly and Orr.

1896: Kelly and Sticht
Erect a three-storey smelting shed
two blast furnaces, 250-foot flue
and chimney stack.

The furnace is lit.

Rush I

Miss! Miss! Are you SURE
this isn't REAL gold?

I am a guide
at the mining and geological museum.
The school holiday program this year
is GOLD!!

A modern prospector
shows pictures of the treasures he has found.
Demonstrates his tools, his skills.

We roll out plastic tubs of water on castors
distribute pre-loaded pans of dirt.
Brass granules have the right specific gravity.
The kids try their hand.

Miss! Miss! There wasn't any gold in my pan!
Mine neither, Miss!

I swirl and agitate
swirl and agitate
until every child
has a prize.

Rush II

        A trickle of expeditioners and track cutters into the valleys.
          A surge of slab huts and prospectors' diggings.
             Torrents of company cottages,
                 sheds, brickworks
                 sleepers and rails
                    chimneys
                     cobbles
                      stacks
                       rush
                      up to
                     heights
                      where
                       ice
                     used
                       to
                       be

Smoke

mine
and smelter
employ
2000 men
use
1000 tonnes
of timber
per
week
not
counting
the railway
sleepers
or the
wood
that fuels
the
locomotive
boilers

．

King Billy
Eucalyptus
Celerytop
Myrtle

．

Once
impervious
forest
comes
down

．

goes
up

Demands

Yellowed and sulphurous the invisible hand
reaches out from the stacks
to scour trees from the hills, a brazen display
of supply and demand.

The Queen grows thick and grey with tailings.
Metal, slag and acid. In her viscid gown
She processes through town
a corrupt monarch demanding tributes.

First she takes the child who runs too fast
to catch her runaway ball.
Then the burly miner who risks his all
and wades in to save her.

His knees buckle, body folds
is sucked below the surface, consumed
by the Queen's corrosive flow
industrial-strength digestion.

Disappearances II

History rarely enters
the settlers' huts
and miners' shacks.

Skirt hems and petticoats
sweep away all footprints
erase all tracks.

I stand on the threshold
dazzled by the outside light
straining to make out shapes
in the shadowy corners.

Before my eyes can adjust
the curtains whisk closed.
The door slams shut.

GIRL

Gert

> 'The fortunes of any mining township are proverbially uncertain, but never in the history of that branch of industry in Tasmania has there been such an awfully sudden collapse as that which is now overwhelming the once thriving centre of Crotty.... the result is a pitiable condition of things, 300 men thrown into idleness'
>
> Launceston Examiner, 2 June 1903

James Crotty makes a wager
on a top-notch claim for copper.
Dies while raising funds in Mayfair.

His company is under orders
mine and railway under survey
Crown allotments up for sale.

The railway runs, three hotels open.
Crotty grows, smelters ignite—
shut down, bankrupt, two years later.

North Mount Lyell lost the wager
sells the railway, mine and smelters.
Crotty-town is going down.

The single men desert in droves.
Leave for jobs in other towns.
Nothing's left to keep them here.

In 1906 Gertrude Agnes is born
to John and Margaret Brown.
Crotty shrinks around them.

Gert shares a name with Alice Agnes,
ghost-sister who died, an infant
four years before Gert was born.

Two sisters live, three brothers too.
Bodies and souls to keep together.
It's lucky John works on the railway.

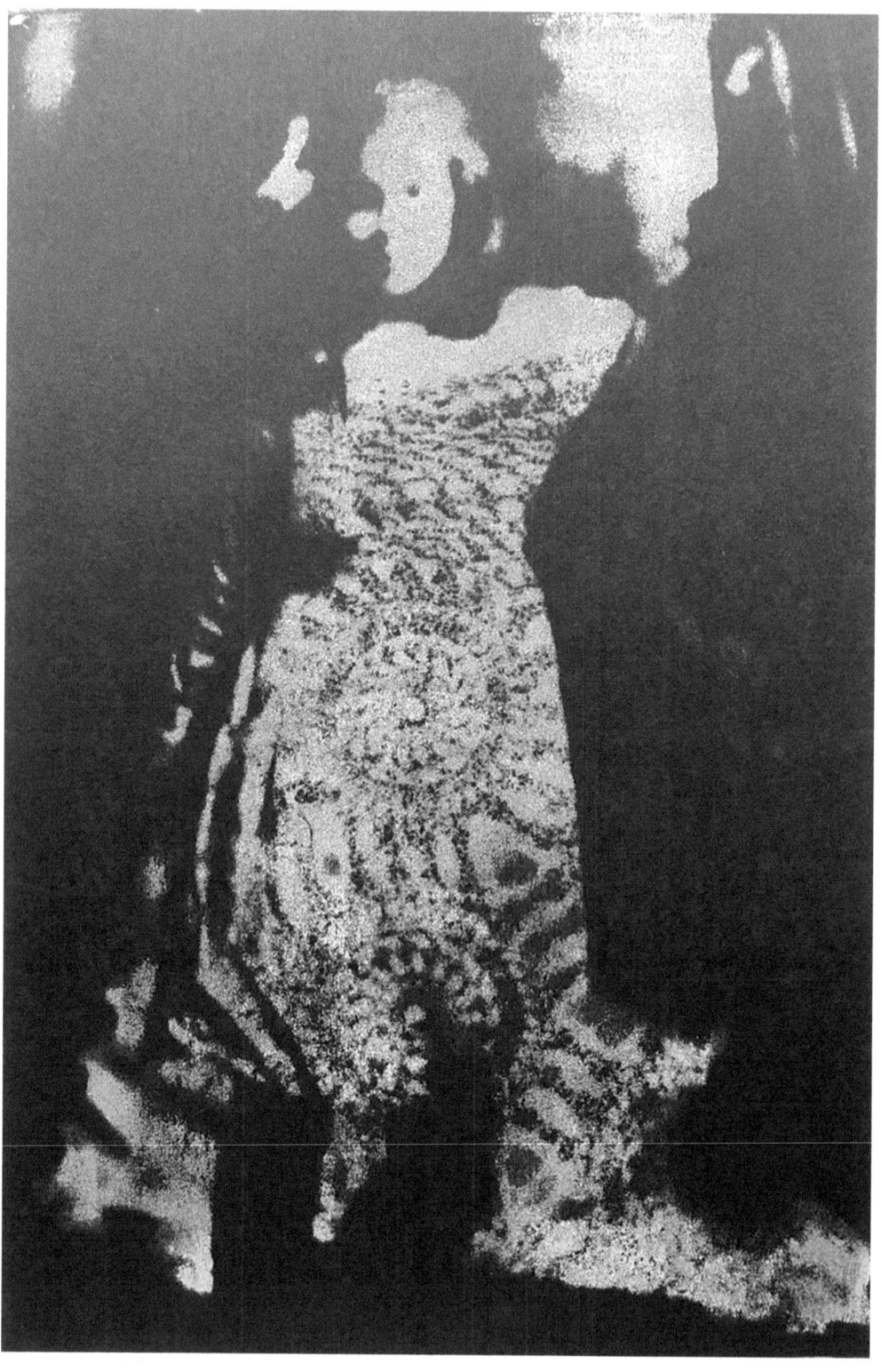

Totality

People look up and tut at the overcast sky.
But in the afternoon the clouds part
frame an azure ground
with vignette of Sun and Moon
in kissing proximity.

The crowd draws a hiss of collective breath
as the air dims to midnight
and the eye of the sky closes
in a long slow wink.

Someone crouches down
holds a pair of smoked glasses
for little Gert to peep at the black moon
with its fringe of coruscating rays.

Night and day.

Then the Sun shoots a bright beam westward
winches herself out of obscurity
sinks languid into the clouds
like an actress leaving the stage
for her pillowy boudoir.

Affinities

In the 1970s
from our house on the mountainside.
I saw the steelworks' sawtooth roofs backlit
by striplight of gleaming sea.
Like cloud machines, chimney stacks
puffed plumes of smoke and steam.

The thing with sulfur
is that soon you don't smell it anymore.
Each morning at four, Bert-next-door
warmed up his four-wheel-drive
and left for his shift down the mine.

Dad trained as a metallurgist.
Managed a factory that made refractories
bricks for kilns and furnaces.
Our garden paths were paved
with arch brick rejects
laid in subtle undulations.

The factory was an obstacle course
of metal rails, stairs and catwalks
smelling of warm minerals and sinter.
Hard-hatted men in high glass boxes
choreographed kiln cars, cranes, mixers and presses.
Fire winked gold in alchemical crevices.

A Sunday drive might go west up the mine-riddled mountain
or south round the port to watch the coal loaders turning
like grotty fairground rides
and the pyrotechnics when the coke ovens poured
or north past miners' cottages clinging to the cliffs
to watch hang-gliders harry Bald Hill's naked pate.

In high school we put on helmets to descend
into Wongawilli colliery on safety-yellow railman cars.
Among glinting black pillars, they turned out the lights.
You could have poked me right in the eye
and I wouldn't have seen it coming.

These places get into you.

We blew out black snot for days.

Fortys—a good old miners game

There is a wager, a facing off against fate.
Is this where a man might find his fortune?
The game is played with a regular deck
and a joker.

Spades.

The deal starts with the eldest hand
and the winch turns, dealing three
and then two, descending
foot by foot into the earth to dig.
The trump card is face up—
shows what he will win if he braves the dark
and the various damps. Of course, any ace
is claimed by the dealer before play starts.

Diamonds.

The North Mount Lyell Company deals,
has bet on profits over safety and
the other players must follow suit.
There is no emergency alarm, accidents are
an ordinary event. Tricks are played
and won—and played and won and played.
And one day lost. Stealthy, greedy for air
a fire breaks out in the Level 2 pump station
700 feet down.

Clubs.

The fire leads trumps, 73 men escape
that first day, 97 more are trapped
or dead. This is a different game now
a game of speed, and the stakes are lives.
S.S. Loongana brings rescue gear from Bendigo
sets a new record across Bass Strait.
Down below, men that could escape go back.
Try to save their mates and don't return.

Days in the dark tick by, and Joe writes a note
to Agnes and his Lorna, pulls the spider
holding the candle-stub from the stope wall
to pin the paper scrap to his shirt.

Hearts

100 hours after the shift went down
the last survivors are brought up.
They managed to renege somehow
until the trumps were exhausted.

The 42 dead are laid face-up
in coffins, ready for
the longest funeral train
in the island's history.
When the ace of hearts is led
you must play a heart
if you hold one.

Bonus tricks

Thank the lord the fire didn't take 45
the score to win
so a new round begins.
The survivors' lungs are ravaged.
A count back would reveal
the real winner.

Fifteen

Gert has a voice.

At a recital in Strahan
she catches the ear
of a music man
from Hobart.

He wants to take her over east
to train as a singer.
Professional.

She will sometimes wonder:
what is that other Gert up to?
The one who said yes?

Bob

Gert's curly hair
hangs right down her back.
Long, brown and lustrous
That is a fact.

The envy of her friends
who wish theirs looked like that.
But she wants to be a modern girl—
hack, hack, hack!

Out of shot

Gert is the girl with dead birds
dangling from her hands. Sport? Pests?
Worth a picture either way.

Ruffled breast feathers.
Scraps and scrapings of beak and claw.
Starbursts of pale underwing.

Through his glass eye, the photographer
observes the serious boy holding gun
as perch for a living bird. Decoy? Pet?

That's Ted Street.
He takes another photograph.
This time Gert is out of shot.

Cliff Bradshaw, capable
in ammunition belt and rolled sleeves
holds gun and bird one-handed.

Ted Street leans into frame.
They say he has a photographic memory.
One look and he can recite a book backwards.

His schoolteacher doesn't like
to be shown up. Asserts himself
through tactical humiliation.

At seventeen, Ted takes his gun
and saves his teacher the trouble.
Point blank. Starburst. Pale underwing.

Cliff

Cliff comes for meals
at her mother's boarding house
where Gert helps out.

With parents dead when he was ten
Cliff came from the mainland
to live with his uncle Fred.
Left school at thirteen for the bakehouse
then menswear, now the railway.

Clean-shaven, competent, affable.
The son of a piano tuner, he's musical too.
Can put his hand to anything.
Is willing to take a risk.

She can talk with him
like she can't talk with anyone else.

In Linda, at her sister Rita's house,
they take their vows

NORTH LYELL HOTEL, LINDA VALLEY 1926. L TO R, MRS GEORGE STOKOE NEE MAGGIE MADDEN, BLUEY STOREY, COLGAN, CLIFF BRADSHAW. FRONT ROW, LEFT TO R, IRENE STOKOE, MRS C BRADSHAW NEE GERT BROWN, MAY CORKERY, BILL STOKOE. MRS. C. BRADSHAW HAD A FAMILY OF 8 DAUGHTERS & 4 SONS. THEY ARE ALL VERY GOOD TO MOTHER. MOTHER WILL GO FOR MILES TO HAVE A GAME OF FORTYS, GOOD OLD MINERS GAME. THOSE DAYS THEY WORKED HARD & EAT WELL & WENT IN FOR HEAVY CORPORAL PUNISHMENT & WENT TO BED EARLY.

Cooking lessons

Cliff takes the licence
of the North Lyell Hotel.
Gert can't cook to save herself
but now she learns
fast, and on the job.
She gets better
and then good.

When she's expecting their first
they leave the pub.
Gert's teetotal,
Doesn't want to raise children there
but she can teach them
how to cook.

Settlement

Cliff goes underground
but the pit doesn't suit him.
He is an outdoors man.

They lease a plot of land
six miles out
on the Princess River.

Cliff goes woodcutting.
Builds a shack. They forget
to move back into town.

Open fire
wood stove
one baby
then another
and another.

Carpenters come to add kitchen
and laundry, bathroom and toilet.
Shack.
House.
Home.

The Hydro

            the invisible dam
            always looms

            the hydro
            reserved this land
        in 1917
        won't put the power on
        in case they refuse to leave
        so it's tilly lamps
    candles
    a chip heater to fill the bath

        the hydro keeps a narrow shack
            on my bank to keep track of me
                how high or low
                    quick or slow
                        my moods and changes
                            flowing lapping trickling rippling seeping
                                sometimes a man comes
                                    to read the gauges

                                    they plan one day
                                    to lock me in concrete
                                    put me to work
                                pushing turbines

Off the record

I google Gert Bradshaw nee Brown.

I soon find Cliff:
Adventurer, expeditioning with Fred Smithies
Civic leader, Council warden for Gormanston.

Gert?

A few fragments:
her name handwritten
in an index of birth certificates.
Photograph in the State Library
deposited by a distant relative.

Back at the Galley
a chatty guide tells me
I will likely find Gert's eldest, Bern
now in his nineties
out at the mill.

At Lynchford there are sheds
piles of twisted silver logs
a high chain mesh fence
topped with barbs
barking dogs.

There is no sign
but this must be it?

I don't go in.

I post Bern a card.

One day my phone rings.

MOTHER

Twelve

>
> Bernard
> Geraldine Colina
> Henry Kay Janice Leslie
> Lynn Norman Gay Lana Lee
> Across eighteen years Gert is gravid
> for nine, will miss the wedding of
> her first-born while she labours
> with the last. It is just as well
> they are all very good
> to Mother.

I wonder

What did you know?
Was it easier or harder
than you expected?
Were your labours quick or slow?
Were there miscarriages
close calls, complications?
Were you dragged inside out?
Or did it seem
like you were
made for this?

The cords are cut at birth
but do they ever
stop tugging?

School bus

Bern is five years old—
Big enough for school, but
six miles to Gormanston
is far too far for little legs.

Gert sends him to live
in Queenstown with Granny
and Grandad Brown
and his three bachelor uncles
who chase the devil out of him!

At last the village gets a school bus
and Bern comes home to his mother.
In a handful of years, legs longer, arms stronger
Grade 7 Merit Certificate accomplished
Bern leaves school to cut timber.

Mother Mine

Forget the government over east in Hobart.
They can't even finish the west coast road.
The only way to get here is by horse, boat
or shanks's pony.

It is the North Mt Lyell Company
that builds houses, offers jobs
in the mine and smelter
cheap food after the war
builds the dam at Lake Margaret
for power and lights.

It is the North Mt Lyell Company
that gets Queenstown through the bottom-out
of the copper price.

Provides a lifeline
before the highway.

Sunny

Gert
is my cheerful
neighbour flowing lapping
trickling rippling seeping
reliable as the
sun

Cliff
is a comet
in an orbit
vigorous
and elliptical
swings in close
manages the mill
makes music under the big willow
plays cards with Gert after tea

then like a rock from a slingshot
 is off cutting timber on the range
  out on construction jobs for days
    business trips up north or over east
      expeditions with Smithies up Frenchman's Cap
            then overland through unmapped country
                    all the way to Cradle Mountain

Gert
keeps home fires
burning children warm
and dry village green
and growing

Fantasy I

My mind follows its fancy
that after the photo with the cockatoos
Gert swaps her t-strap shoes
for boots, adorns her curly hair
with King Billy seed cones, scents it
with leatherwood blossom.

That Gert, so arrayed
takes the double-barrel gun on one shoulder
black cockatoo on the other
and strides away through the button grass
thylacine by her side.

Essentials

The Great Depression is gnawing on the island,
sucking out its marrow and what little fat it has.
If you don't have a dollar in your hand, you'll starve.
Try and survive on trapped rabbits.

A stream of people stumbles in on foot,
tumbling down the hill to the village.

Gert makes them food. Cliff gives them tea,
sugar, a billy and blanket. A shed to sleep in,
the dignity of work. Later, he saves Italians
from internment by the same strategy.

Some move on when they can, some stay.

Cliff meets old prospectors and drovers
on the ranges. They trust him
with their money, come in to the Princess
when they can't work the hills anymore.

Butcher-turned prospector Alec Maywood.
Giant Jim Adams, six-foot-six.
They collect firewood, labour in the garden.
Treat the children like their own grandbabies.

Teach them essential skills, like
how to kill and pluck a chicken

The mill

Cliff buys Morrison's sawmill.
Moves it upriver from
the mouth of the King.
The boiler chimney towers
over the house.

They grease the gears.
Light the fire, stoke the boiler.
Start the hiss and sigh of steam
chugga-chugga of pistons
rumble and rattle of belts and wheels
the blade's whine and scream.

Roll a log onto the carriage.
Align the grain, make the iron jaws bite.
Set the depth of the cut with a lever
and send the carriage forward and back
to drive log against savage circle of teeth.

Carry away the golden slab.
Stack it to dry with the others.
Savour the smells of sawdust and sap.
Oil and grease. Shovel the scraps back
into the belly of the beast.

Set the next cut.

A tight team

Everyone has their chores
and no mucking about.
Curse or swear and Gert'll
threaten to wash your mouth out.
Cliff permits no talk at the table
until the eating is done—believes
it interferes with digestion, or perhaps
he just likes his peace.

Forget to stack dry wood
for Gert's breakfast fire,
and make no mistake,
Cliff'll get you up out of bed
to finish the job at midnight.

When the evening meal is done,
the kitchen tidied, children in bed
the cards come out.

Gert tells Cliff about her days
in the house by the river
the eddies and pools of the domestic
her trips over to town.

Cliff tells Gert about
the work and the men
how the boys are coming on.
About crossing the ranges
with the string of draught horses.
How they track a thylacine
through the snow.

Plenty

They have few store-bought things, not much waste.
They have space. The river. A cow or two.
A pantry full of fruit and vegetables from the garden,
sacks of potatoes, bottles and jars of preserves
and pickles, butter, milk and cream.
Eggs dipped in yellow wax, nestled
in boxes of sawdust to keep.
Clothes, hand-sewn or knitted.
Brothers and sisters.
Work. Laughter. Adventures.
Freedom.

Music and Pictures

Gert's brother Harry has a motor car.
Once a fortnight he drives the family
to the pictures. They cram in and sing
all the way there

> *Goodbye, Piccadilly*
> *Farewell Leicester Square*
> *It's a long, long way to Tipperary*
> *But my heart's right there*

all the way back

> *Keep the Home Fires Burning,*
> *While your hearts are yearning.*
> *Though your lads are far away*
> *They dream of home.*

Flood and freeze

when rains come
    copious i grow
        rise and quicken
            flowing lapping trickling rippling seeping
                      overflow my limits
                            creep across the road
                                shallow then deep
                                    they bring out the tinnie
                                      to meet the school bus

                                    in deepest winter i slow
                                go crystalline, freeze
                              the children skate over me
                            on empty powdered milk cans
                        strapped to booted feet
                  slide fall laugh
            sometimes cry
      pick themselves and one another up
    their momentum carries them
  their brake
my bank

Satellite

Sometimes the siblings walk upriver to the Eldon ranges
or as far as the Raglans (if the timber cutters aren't there).
A ground sheet, tarp to make a lean-to.
Matches, sausages, potatoes.
Their very own village for a few nights.

Perpetual motion

i am perpetual motion

flowing lapping trickling rippling seeping
flowing lapping trickling rippling seeping

like me
the people who live on my bank
   are rarely still
      waking yawning walking running
         sawing chopping cutting digging
            playing teasing joking eating

Gert
is the mother
is always in motion
lighting kindling tending measuring
chopping stirring pouring cracking
wiping sweeping washing bathing
dressing cleaning combing nursing
baking feeding planting growing
harvesting weeding drying bottling
scolding baking milking churning
sewing mending knitting eating
singing laughing weeping
sleeping

Gert
   is like the pebble
      circling in my current
         slowly carving its niche
            in the stone of my bed
         always moving
            always still
         while the current
            of the river
         the family
            flows
            around
            her

Beef and vegetables

Wild cows are in the garden—
again! Gert can't harvest a tomato
or hang out the wash
without risking a charge.

Great-great-grand-calves
of the herd that fed the workers
on the West Coast road, plus
descendants of Cliff's old mob.

Down from the Eldon ranges
they graze the tender lettuces
trample the spinach and parsnips
drop sloppy pats in every path.

They are big, stroppy, dangerous.
An overhead shot will send them off
but when a beast looks fit for the table
Alec Maywood shoots to kill.

Then Gert's high-carbon-steel knife
forged in the mine, cuts precisely
along the dotted lines
her mind's eye draws
beneath the hide.

Intimate things

In Gert's family, they didn't talk
about intimate things.
So she didn't learn how.

The boys, she can leave to Cliff.
The girls too, for some things
but not others.

Her eldest, she tells
what she must
what she can.

Is relieved that, once given
the secret knowledge will flow
like water spilled downhill
from older to younger
one sister to another.

Quiet

They say Gert was 'quiet-living'
Does this mean private?
Am I prying?
Would Gert want her story told?
Like this?
By me?
What would she think?
What will they think?

Good Times

Queenstown. Gormanston. Linda.
Not uncivilised clusters of shacks
and huts and grime and grind and vice.
Well—not all the time.

These are boom towns!
People up on their luck towns!
Know how to have fun towns!
And if you can't find it, make it.

There are more pubs than you can
down a drink at—though some
make the attempt. But also
a library, gymnastic club, cinema

institute, dance hall, choirs
football club, roller-skating rink!
There are bands and orchestras
debutante balls, costume parties.

Parades to celebrate important days.
To farewell the lads who enlist.
Welcome back the shrunken number
of shrunken men who return.

Gramophone

the music they make
    with instruments
        and voices
            alive as my water
                flowing lapping trickling rippling seeping
                  but sometimes the wavering voice
            of a gramophone
      spills out the window
     trickles down to my banks
Gert trills along

> *Between two trees there lies a story true,*
> *A story true that I will tell to you.*
> *'Twas there that I first fell in love with you;*
> *Your hair was gold, your eyes were blue.*
>
> *Between two trees we kissed as lovers do,*
> *As lovers do who know their love is true.*
> *We carved a heart, a heart within each tree;*
> *A heart for you, a heart for me.*
>
> *And when we wed, we wed between the trees,*
> *Beneath the trees we vowed eternity.*
> *The trees looked down and smiled as though to say,*
> *'God bless your love upon this wedding day'.*

Jack and May

Cliff's brother Jack plays the piano
tells tall tales, a born entertainer.
He marries May, who draws her mouth on
big and red like a film star
dangles a cigarette from her lips.

They both enjoy a tipple, and
to niggle one another. Jack has
a drink, a dig, winds her up.
May tips a dish of custard or stew
over his head more than once.
Gert disapproves, but can't
hide her smile entirely.

At a dance, May is ready to leave.
Jack is still drinking with a mate
so May issues her ultimatum, storms away
swears she'll walk the six miles home.

When they catch her up in the car
she has made a good start, breathing clouds
heels striking sparks as she marches up the hill
towards the stars.

Left and Right

Gert votes Liberal
but her brother Tom
is a Labor man.
They like to squabble
about politics.

Before long,
Tom's wife Beattie wishes
that their heads held
neither ideas
nor tongues.

Full stop

Sometimes Gert takes a holiday
in the city at a hotel
where the room is cleaned
the food is cooked
everything is provided.
She wears good frocks and jewels.
The only time she stops.

Back at the Princess
her daughters keep the household
flowing.

Fantasy II

With her parents' blessing
Gert went to study in Hobart
with the music man.

Don't you remember
Nellie Melba
Ella Caspers
Florrie Forde
Gladys Moncrieff
the McKean Sisters
sweet Gertie Brown?

Shindig

It is Christmas—start of
three weeks' holiday.

In the shade of the big willow
Gert and the girls lay tables
ready for a congregation.
Cliff puts on a barrel of beer
bottles of wine
cordial for the kids.

After roast dinners at home
the loggers, saw-millers, labourers
and their families come over.

They stretch out
with the long summer evening.
Replete.

The sky colours and dims
fills with conversation.

With moon rise for spotlight
they take their turn as entertainers
share a song, story, dance
or party trick.

Jack plays the piano, Curly
his mouth organ, Cliff the flute.

Everybody sings.

Selective

'Never put an axe or drill into a tree
you aren't going to take'
says Cliff.

Some trees are so massive
you can't put an axe
into girth like that.

So wind the augur.
Pour in some black powder.
Slide in a fuse.
Tap in a plug.
Strike a match.

Boom

Crack

In an instant
thousands of years
are snapped open
to reveal the golden
heart.

Split in two, it might still be
too big for the truck.
Might need another blast
to bring it down to scale.

Tyres bulge
and brake fluid boils
as they inch down
the mountain.

Back at the mill
it might take a week
(as long as creation)
to dismember this
cellulose colossus.

No ventriloquist

No first-person account
self-portrait from the interior
diary
journal
letters.

If they exist
it might be prying
to read words not meant
for me.

No.

To impersonate

you

would be impertinent
to inflate
your form
with my breath
put words in

your mouth

wrap

your skin

around mine
reanimate

you

with my
alien imagination
from another
place and time.

I write around
you.
Hope for

your
faint apparition

in the space
on the page.

MATRIARCH

Welcome

                    high-pitched voices
               a fresh cascade of children
        flowing lapping trickling rippling seeping

       they splash
      in my water
     bounce on the
    make-do trampoline
   of the turkey run
  shout for a ride
on the old Bren Gun
  excavate Sawdust Mountain
      scale its peak
           stick their heads
                into the exhilarating gale
                       of the sawmill exhaust
                          know to stay well away
                             from the blades

                          are always welcome
                           at the old house
                            among lupins
                        and blackcurrants
                     always have a place
                  with Nan and Pop
              at the table under
          the willow

Addition

>
> DEAD TREES ARE YIELDING
> £20,000 OF TIMBER YEARLY
>
>
> *Cliff Bradshaw, 63, broad-shouldered,*
> *white haired and of middle height*
> *is the head of the family.*
>
> *He has four sons working with him*
> *Bernard, Norman, Leslie and Henry*
> *and three daughters—Lyn, Kay and Colleen.*
>
> *All the family (including Mrs Bradshaw)*
> *have shares in the business, and in addition*
> *the men draw wages.*

Allegiance

Cliff keeps hunting dogs.
Deer hounds, great loping beasts.
Gert does what she must for them
but does not regard them with affection.

She has her own pets:
a King Charles spaniel
a series of yapping corgis
inspired by the Queen.

Convenience

Hot water at a whim
for the washing or a bath!
Light that won't pop and flicker
at the flick of a switch!

The Hydro turns the power on in '76
on strict condition
that everything comes out
when the dam goes in.

Spoil

Someone says Cliff spoils her
with good clothes, a gleaming opal.
Fur coat. A chartered holiday.
Whatever she wants.

> There is spoil
> around here, plenty of it.
>
> Mountains of spoil dug out of mines
> cast out of furnaces, poured into creeks.
>
> Other spoils are hauled to the bank.
>
> Much has been spoiled
> river, hillsides, soil
> full of copper
> aluminium
> zinc.

Gert isn't spoiled by Cliff.
He just likes to treat her.
Treat her right.

The tower

                                                        For six years
                                                        the tower of
                                                        smelter stack
                                                       has pointed at
                                                       the fickle sky
                                                       without   its
                                                       smoky plume
                                                       missing   too
                                                       many   bricks
                                                       must   be
                                                       pushed before
                                                       it fails   falls

                                     ...

           So: the blast
              slow tilt like
                 a clock hand.
                    Does the time
                       seem to move
                          backward or
                             forward? Well
                                it depends on
                                     where you stand.

                                 ...

                           i m p a c t   .
               b r e a k i n g   .   b r i c k s . s m a s h
      .   .   ..
    .. s h u d d e r i n g .. e a r t h .. d u s t .. b l o o m s ..
   .   .   ..
     s e t t l e s   . . r e v e a l s .... . tower ..   .
  . . .... v a n i s h e d ..in   its ..   own   ...
    .. .   p u ff.. .   of s m o k e ..   .

...

	signifies	upside-down			it depends on
the	disaster	inverted	Fortune	does the	where you
Tower in	upheaval	is disaster	lays out	Tower appear	stand.
the tarot deck	broken pride	averted	her cards	upright or fallen?	

Oh dear

Cliff is in the hospital.
Gert has a hotel room
the comfort of her daughter
and the news.

All night she murmurs
Oh dear
Oh dear

When they get home to the Princess
he cuts her a mountain of wood
so she will never need to cut her own.

They both refuse the prognosis
the abjection of the body.

Their golden wedding passes
just before Cliff.

Oh dear

Oh dear.

Piano

The concert piano
Cliff bought in the sixties
broods in a corner of the living room.

Gert hates its domineering ways—
how everyone has to shush when someone plays.
It kills the conversation.

It is the first thing to go.

She can certainly live
without that monstrosity
if she must live
without him.

Fantasy III

Gert needs a distraction
from the sucking void of grief.
Something to keep her
in motion, a new challenge.
One morning she appears at the mill
in Cliff's flat cap and too-big jacket
ready to superintend.
She has raised a dozen children.
How hard can it be?

Gormanston

>When is a person not a person anymore?
>A body not a body? Some organs
>we can live without:
>a limb, an eye or two. A kidney.

>(we might be haunted
>by their phantoms)

>Other parts are vital:
>liver, brain, heart.

Gormanston loses its schools in the fifties
Post Office in seventy-nine.
Houses are hoisted onto flatbeds
trucked away for transplant.
Those left behind flee the desolation.
Struggle as poor relations in bigger towns.

In '86, Gormanston municipality
is engulfed by Queenstown, then
both are swallowed whole by the
whale of the West Coast Council.

The remaining houses fall into dishevelled
neglect. Paint cracks and curls, steel rusts
timbers fray into splinters, the asphalt edges
of the basketball court erode and crumble.

Street signs at night still glimmer
iridescent in headlights.
A few people stay, relish the quiet.
Keep the idea of Gormanston
on life support, pulse fluttering.

Soon

The greenies and Feds
have had their way.
The Gordon below Franklin
has been canned.

The clouds that hung
on the horizon
for all this time
have blown in.

The Hydro brings forward
the King and Anthony scheme.
A resentful state government
approves it in weeks.
A placatory Commonwealth
throws in some dough.

Gert and Cliff knew
this day would come.
But that was before
they built their home,
before their village grew.

Before she knew they
wouldn't face this day
together.

                      soon I will pool
                                spread
                                          lap at the door
                              climb the walls
                     seep into everything
            that they have built
                  everything they don't
                              carry away

Gert won't stay to watch.

The knack

At eighty-two
after a lifetime
—ffff—
of trying
—fffff—fffff—
and failing
blowing air
not notes
Gert purses her lips
and whistles!

She witters away
at all the old songs.

Between two trees
The years have swiftly flown
The trees are bare
And I am all alone
I close the book
My book of memories
Of one who sleeps
Between two trees

What Tasmania stands to lose

The King River
brought the first people
to this valley.
Now it will sink
their memory.

The Tasmanian Aboriginal Centre tells
their story—'*The King River and the Lairmerenga:
What Tasmania Stands to Lose*'.
Calls for a delay in the inundation
so experts can survey
learn what the valley knows
catalogue the artefacts it keeps
before the dammed water
creeps up to submerge
a central vein in understanding
dissolve a *contact link*.
destroy the chance to understand
a people.
their complexity.
their beauty.

The proper order

There is a proper order to things.
No mother should have to go
to her own child's funeral
even when the child is grown.

Geraldine, her eldest girl, goes first.
Then diamond driller Les.

Cliff's funeral seems barely over
though it is a dozen years ago.
Gert carries her man-shaped
life-sized grief.

Now, two more who she bore
is more than she can bear.

The ceremonies go on without her.
Women, who are close, stay with her.

Salvage

        they haul out all they can
            twisted corpses of huon and king billy
                are dragged off the hills
                    out of the valley

            sheds and shacks come down
                then the houses
              the brothers check
              every nook and cranny

                Gert is well-gone
            but their sister won't leave

        on the eve that the dam will be complete
      they arrive to find Lana and her husband
            sitting down to tea

      Bern and Norm take the bed apart
          put it straight on the truck
     so Lana can't lay down her head
   once more and sleep
 to my flowing lapping rippling
trickling seeping

they join her at the table
   the rain is on its way
      it is time to leave
         or drown

Diluvian

The stop-logs drop
with the first winter rain.
The waters rise
without delay.

People watch
from shifting shores.

Other creatures are ambushed
by this unnatural event.
Rangers and volunteers
in boats rescue possums
wallabies, pademelons
lizards, bettongs.

There is no orderly
two-by-two queue.

When a snake flows
over the tinnie's rim
the men jump into
the drink.

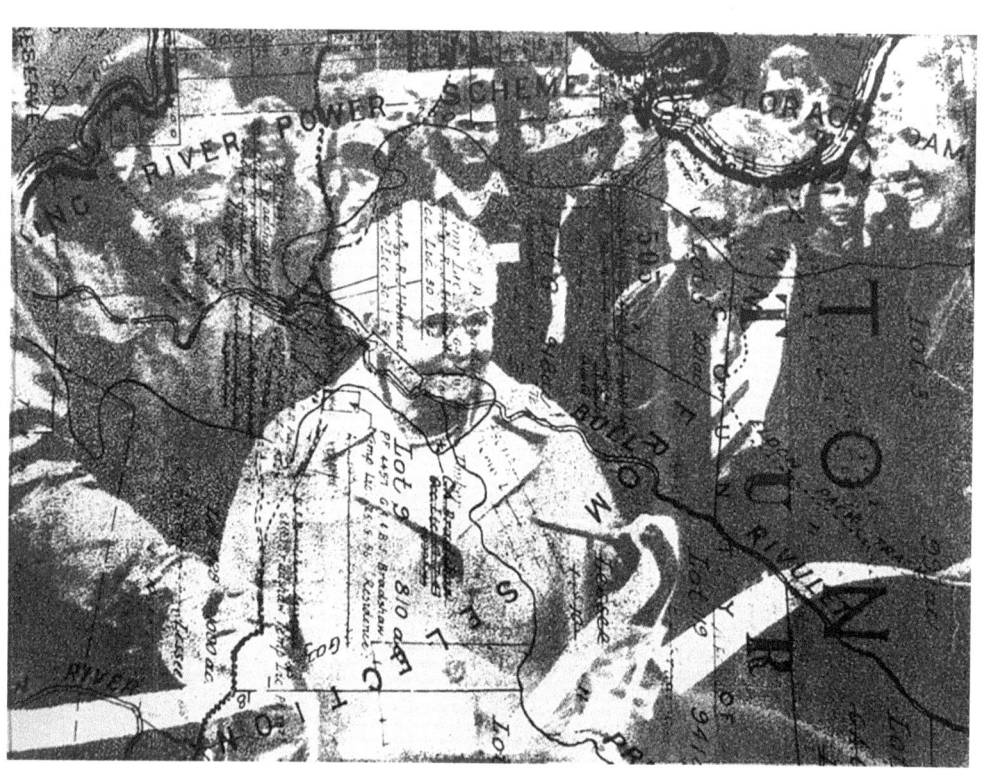

The Bradshaw Bridge

A black ribbon of fresh bitumen
unspools along a contour.

Gert snips the strip of red satin
hung across the concrete span.

The new bridge passes
their small Atlantis.

Gert smiles for the camera.
Wishes Cliff was here to see it.

King River Power Development as Triumphal Corporate Elegy

(Vivaldi's Primavera—strings)

The aquamarine brilliance of Lake Burbury!
The imposing concrete edifice of Crotty Dam!
Exquisite engineering excellence
that is a tunnel under a massive mountain.
A power station named after one of Tasmania's pioneers.
The irresistible meld of modern engineering skill
and plain old hard yakka!

The King River Power Scheme marks
the end of an era. The era of dam building
design and construction achievements
that have made the world sit up and take notice!

(Wagner's 'Hall of the Mountain King'—synths & drum machine)

It is about brave women and men.
It's about people thrown together in communities
who built a comradeship.
It's about doing something that will benefit
thousands of Australians
for decades to come.

(Vivaldi's Primavera—synths)

In 1992, the Crotty dam is finished
standing 80 meters tall!
Lake Burbury spreads out regally
across its 53 square kilometres!

Many of the areas disturbed
are now hidden beneath the surface.

The hydro construction era is drawing to a close.
The King River power development
will stand as a grand memorial.
The King is dead. Long live the King!

Flickering

                    Gert has left me
                  for the Queen
                is settled in town
              in Colville Street
          where everything is handy

lunch with daughters
visits with friends
  weekly massage
    for her bad back
      a thrifty flutter
        on the pokies

            sometimes a win

                in her cottage
                    comfy chair
                        in the flickering light
                          of the telly
                              she casts intricate magic
                                  from her fine hooked wand

                          drifts of lace doilies
                        forming between
                    her flickering
                hands

THEREAFTER

In loving memory

A stiff wind drives
up the Vale of Chamouni
over Linda Pioneer Cemetery.
Over granite headstone
crisply carved as open book.

The left-hand leaf:
'Charles Albert Clifford Bradshaw,
'Cliff' Beloved husband of Gert.
Passed away 4 Dec 1978,
Aged 72 Years'.

Today fresh flowers
bend and tremble.
The smooth right-hand page
waits.

Gertrude Agnes Bradshaw, nee Brown.
1906–2001

Chimera

                              from headwaters
                                        pillowed
                                             against
                                                  the eldon ranges
                                                       a bit of me
                                                  is still flowing
                                             lapping rippling
                                        trickling seeping down
                                   from the high country
                              i curve swerve
                         cascade and riffle
                         babble and chatter
                    agile and rapid
               from
               the mountains
                    flowing
                         lapping
                              rippling
                                   trickling
                                        seeping
at the new dam I am conjoined abruptly with the King and his tributaries stapled together in a crude surgery with concrete and steel my body is slowed swollen and whether our skin glints textured by wind or is mirror-still and sky-like you cannot see through me cannot see that
                                        below
                                             i
                                                  still
                                                       flow
                                                            an undercurrent
                                                                 hidden
                                                                      trickling

Care and maintenance

It's routine. December 2013
Mr Lucas and Mr Gleeson
change flask linkages
on a discharge door cylinder.

They assemble
the temporary platform
used many times before.
Soft King Billy suspended
above 25 metre shaft.
A 'wiggle-test' to check
it is secure.

Safety harnesses
are: recommended
        optional
        inconvenient.

The linkage and arm
on their heavy steel plate
fall a mere half-metre.

The platform proves
its temporary nature
and gives

way

…

In the new year Mr Welsh (aka Digger)
is assigned to bog at the draw point.
Checks for bulging of the mine wall
and when it ticks the boxes, starts
carting out broken rock with
a sixty-plus-tonne loader.

    MUD-RUSH RAMS MASSIVE MACHINE BACKWARDS BURIES AXLES
                        BREAKS WINDOWS CRAMS CAB WITH EARTH

What is a man worth?

The mine is put into
care and maintenance.

Crotty, 2016

             the driest
              October
             on record

         sucked up by
       the sky's crisp sponge
       lake burbury gives its ghosts
       a breather

       shrinkage rings graph
       the diminishing reservoir
       foliage and flesh long gone
       the forest's exposed bones
       rattle in the wind.

   brick foundations are divulged
    beams and bottles
      furnaces that have smelted mud
         for twenty years.

           birds flit in and out of windows
               where trout and galaxias darted.

                 soon we rivers
                        will take them back.

Bread

Unconformity: old and new
sometimes uncomfortably cheek-by-jowl.

BREAD AND CIRCUSES!
shouts the banner on the pub.
REOPEN THE MINE!

Is this festival palaver a big fat
distraction from the facts?
This town needs jobs, industry
has never done anything else.

Prices are up.
Nice if you are selling.
Tough if you are renting
and there is nowhere
cheaper
to go.

Reading list

This is a space
for the Palawa

space for you
to find them
read their stories

Walter George Arthur
Joel Stephen Birnie
Karen Brown
Thomas Brune
Joyce Cameron
Patsy Cameron
Jim Everett-puralia meenamatta
Dave mangenner Gough
Julie Gough
Rex Greeno
Greg Lehman
Neika Leurenna Warrane Lehman
Kartanya Maynard
Nathan Maynard
Sharnie Read
Theresa Sainty
Nunami Sculthorpe-Green
Adam Thompson
Luana Towney
Errol West
Ida West

those I haven't found
those yet unknown
those to come

Rings and ripples

```
                                    Hannah
                              Koby        Shontaye
                          Blair               ***
                       Riley              Alec
                   Zarnah      Matt Kirsty Mark    Jordan
                Oliver     Samantha    Kimberly      Jhye
             Cruz       Lucas              Cindy      Jack
             ***     Manisha                Kate      ***
          Cale       Joel                   Mick     Levi
                  Wayne          Dean       Leonie   Luke
                   ***        Brooke Jason Tina     Naomi
              Ben              Franc        Nicki  Shahnina
           Nathan             John           Ian     ***
           Ellie            Jeaneane         Kim    Cameron
         Samuel             Robyn      Bern       Sean    Kelly
          Amy               Curtis   Geraldine  Colina   Wanita    Zac
         Kate               David      Kay                Vic     Angie
          ***                Jan              Gert   Henry  Mark  Kade
                           Wayne    Harry      &           Noel    Ada
         Jack               Jon     Norm      Cliff   Lana  Linda  Max
         Jesse             Albin   Janice           Leslie Kerryn Sasha
          ***             Adrian          Lynn       Gay    Lisa Ricarda
              Kristi      Jodi              Lee            Peta    ***
              Callum      Alan                        Tracey      Latham
               Teghan            Andrew              Roxie       Isabella
                Felicity         Joanne              Paul         Hayley
                 Brandi           Peter             Kylie       Alexandra
                  Kirsty                          Dominic         Stuart
            Eli    Tylor                                    Aaron    ***
              Arty        Lucas                             Adam    Lily
                   Gracie       Claire                    Jordan    Ella
                    ***         Teanne                      ***    Caleb
                     Egan            Bethany              Jason    Riley
                       Lydia            Joel Kelli Sam              ***
                         Aliegha                            Edward
                            Mikayla                         Millie
                                     ***                    Dustin
                                   Emily   Hollie
```

Δelta

```
                              the
                              mine
                           is closed
                          eroded soil
                        exposes bedrock
                      sulphur-rich igneous
                    pyrite.  the rain falls pure
                   but leaches    metal sulphides
                 into the creek   down to the Queen
                she is rich   with    cobalt   aluminium
              copper zinc iron   still nips any impertinent
           life    in the     bud    with     acid tongue
          at her   confluence    with    the King   her rust-red
        waters   billow  veils  ribbons  in his clear    dark flow
       he    picks up    some of her load    carries    heavy metals
      many       miles       deposits     a delta in   Macquarie Harbour
     under      fetid                        fish                    farms
    unless     the mine                    is forced                to pay
   what        will                         change                    ?
```

Trees on the moon

Barely perceptible bum-fluff
tints the naked ranges.
Verdant five-o'clock-shadow
of stiff radiata bristles or
pliant whiskers of grass
over gaunt cheekbones
chalky white, pink
and ochre yellow.

Some welcome it, others mourn.
The place they knew
is leaving them, their singular scenery
lapsing into ordinary.

There are rumours of night-time parties
going out to weed under cover of dark.
Without acid rain's long blade
they work in vain.

Sprouts and saplings snag dirt and leaves.
Something like soil accumulates, kindles seed.
Away from tailings and leachate, microorganisms
and shy invertebrates flourish and breed.

Older folk reminisce about the moonscape
sunset's mimic, radiant
in the golden hour.

> Not everything will keep.
> Not everything should be kept.
>
> Clouds of DDT on the beach
> Agent Orange, atomic bombs
> asbestos mines, acid rain
> scoured mountains
> and other regrettable souvenirs
> of the 20th century.
>
> Keep stories, photographs, films
> paintings, memories.

A new forest is on its way.

Power

This island boasts 100 per cent
renewable electricity.

*Our renewable status would not have been possible without the ingenuity and
courage of the Tasmanians who helped create our culture and society.*

With its self-sufficiency
this island aspires to be
the nation's battery.

*There are social licence challenges
concerns about environmental impacts
of renewable energy developments
not required to supply Tasmania*

This island accounts for
40 per cent of the nation's
native forest log volume.

In 21-22 a third of this island's
5.225 million tonnes of wood fibre
came from native forests.

*Don't put a drill or a saw into a tree
you aren't going to take
said Cliff*

Less than one per cent
of logged native forest volume
finishes as sawn timber.

Custodian

In flannel and work boots
he guards the trove of timber.

Pilgrims and petitioners
come to plead their case.

A fiddle? A mandolin?
The exuberant soul of the once-living tree
so vivid it might stand up and dance?

They must have something fine in mind
the words to describe it, the skills
to manifest their vision.

Nothing less will satisfy.

Commonplace

This place is common.
This story is miraculous.
This place is not history.
This story is not fable.
This place is not a lesson.
This story has no moral.
This place is a microcosm.
This story isn't finished.
This place is a community.
This story is fiction.
This place is a future.
This story is true.
This place is miraculous.
This story is common.

EPILOGUE

The Queen runs clear

at an indeterminate time
        in a future you can't yet imagine
                the earth has done her work

                      flowing lapping rippling trickling seeping

                          perhaps you humans have helped her
                            perhaps there are none of you left

                            the final spoil is locked in rocks
                          no longer weeping, seeping
                      wounds and scars are dressed
                with fertile soil

              through
          the circle of time
        the serpentine Queen
    bites her own tail

now as clear
  as she was before
     her middle age
        of muddy grey
           of rust-red sludge

                as if young again
                she carries
                  life

Coda

We count time by hours, the spin and circle of our small planet.
But some things might be better measured by the
slow-swirling arms of this spiral galaxy
or the cycles of the universe
gasping matter into
one dense
point
.
then
blowing it out into

g l i t t e r i n g   c h a o s

Acknowledgements

I first must thank the members of the Bradshaw family who shared their memories, stories and photographs of Gert, as well as their time, hospitality and enthusiasm for the project. Many of the poems in this collection are based on the recollections of Bern Bradshaw, Norman and Sue Bradshaw, Gay Bon and Ian Bradshaw. Special thanks to Ian for his encouragement and support.

Thanks to the Galley Museum in Queenstown, where I saw the two photographs of Gert which caught my attention back in 2018 and piqued the fascination that became this project. Also to the late Eric Thomas who founded the museum, and whose lively typewritten captions contributed greatly to the allure of those photographs. The Museum volunteers were always hospitable and generous with the Museum's artefacts, and their prompt permission to freely use images and material from the museum collection was a boon.

Thanks to Zara Trihey for her hospitality and warmth in Queenstown, and to Peter Miller and the Peanut for a great day out on Lake Burbury to meet the Princess River.

Queenstown Library also provided a valuable local history collection and a warm and comfortable place to work.

Thank you to the early readers of individual poems or the developing collection. They include Ella Kurz, Melinda Smith, Es Foong and my creative research teacher Ruth Hadlow and my classmates.

Thanks to Penelope Layland and Michael Wellham, who offered me a base in Tasmania for periods of research and writing. And special thanks to Penelope for her thoughtful and generous work as editor of this collection.

Thanks to the ACT Government for the Arts Activities Grant that bought me time to complete the manuscript that became *GERT*.

And finally, thank you to Shane Strange of Recent Work Press, for his skill, work and care in turning this work into a beautiful publication

Supported by

Endnotes

Prologue

p. 5: 'In the Galley Museum, Queenstown, Tasmania 2018'
Written in response to the striking photograph, reproduced on page 4 with thanks to the Eric Thomas Galley Museum in Queenstown.

As well as being the place where I encountered the images that initiated this project, the Galley Museum collection has extensively informed this work, and the source of a number of images used in the artwork, as noted in the image list.

The Eric Thomas Galley Museum in Queenstown is housed in the original Imperial Hotel, built in 1897. The museum was first established by Mr Eric Thomas, who moved to Queenstown in 1932 and opened the first displays in 1972–3. He collected the more than 1,000 photographs on display, the captions of which reflect his extensive local knowledge. The museum includes 30 rooms that also feature historical items such as personal effects, documents, cameras, theatre projectors, household items, gems and minerals, military, emergency services, and mining artifacts.

Formation

p. 11: 'Terrain'
The details in this poem draw on 'Child of Gondwana: The Geological Making of Tasmania' by Keith Corbett. Forty-South Publishing, 2019.

p. 13: 'Discovery'
'Electric sky waves veils of colour across the stars'— '41,000 years ago, people in Tasmania must have seen spectacular auroras when the Earth's magnetic field flipped, and for a few thousand years, north was south and south was north'. Research published in the journal Quaternary Geochronology, accessed via University of Melbourne: https://www.unimelb.edu.au/newsroom/news/2021/february/first-humans-in-tasmania-must-have-seen-spectacular-auroras

Palawa Aboriginal stories from Tasmania recalling the creation of Bass Strait 12,000 years ago and the presence of a bright southenrn star may be among the oldest recorded stories in the world: https://www.unimelb.edu.au/newsroom/news/2023/august/tasmanian-aboriginal-oral-traditions-among-the-oldest-recorded-narratives

p. 16: 'The Lairmerenga'
Draws from information in "The King River and the Lairmerenga—what Tasmania Stands to Lose', Tasmanian Aboriginal Centre, 1991.

p. 20: 'Arrivals'
Surveyor-General James Erskine Calder (1808–1882) came to Tasmania from England in 1829, and led many expeditions. His prolific writing provides valuable records of early settler exploration of Lutruwita, noting that the author found his views on Aboriginal people abhorrent.

p. 21: 'Naming and Taming'

Observations in italics are drawn from Calder, James Erskine, 1808–1882. Recollections of Sir John & Lady Jane Franklin in Tasmania. Sullivan's Cove, Adelaide, 1984. Originally published in six parts in the Tasmanian Tribune in October 1875.

p. 25: 'Crucible'

Dates and events are drawn from 'KING—story of a river' by Patsy Crawford. Montpellier Press, 2000.

p. 29: 'Smoke'

Data drawn from Eric Thomas' caption of photograph of wood cutters, Galley Museum, Queenstown.

p. 31: 'Demands'

The episode in the third and fourth stanza is based loosely on an incident related by Thomas Courto in 'Queenstown: the way we were : short stories and verse including Freddy—the boy that became a man'. Manuta Tunapee Puggaluggalia Publishers, 2005.

Girl

p. 35: 'Gert'

Quote from Launceston Examiner, 2 June 1903 accessed via Trove: https://trove.nla.gov.au/newspaper/article/35548769

Family oral history indicates that Gert was born in Crotty, however her birthplace is registered as Gormanston. Link to record: https://libraries.tas.gov.au/Digital/RGD33-4-18/58E17615-490E-42DF-A9F7-6AB31476003E

p. 37: 'Totality'
There is no evidence four-year-old Gert saw the total eclipse in May 1910, but it is possible. Queenstown was one of few places in the world where this eclipse was observed, as described in the diaries of Rev. Leslie S. Macdougall (http://macdougalldiaries.blogspot.com/2012/08/solar-eclipse-of-sun-9-may-1910.html) and an account by Charles P Buter published in Nature on 6 July 1911: https://www.nature.com/articles/087024a0

p. 41: 'Fortys—a good old miners game'

For this piece, I drew on 'A Tasmanian Tragedy—Disaster at Mt Lyell' by T R Mackay, on the Australasian Mining Safety Journal website: https://www.amsj.com.au/a-tasmanian-tragedy-disaster-at-mt-lyell/.

I used Wikipedia's description of the rules for 'Forty-Fives', a card game also known as 'Fortys' in some mining communities including on Tasmania's West Coast. Thanks to Ian Bradshaw for confirming that Fortys and Forty-fives are the same game. Eric Thomas' caption of Gert, Cliff and others on the verandah of the North Lyell Hotel includes 'Mother (Gert) will go a long way for a game of Fortys, good old miners game'. (see page 52)

p. 49: 'Out of Shot'

This account of Ted Street is based on an anecdote related by Norman Bradshaw.

Mother

p.61: 'Twelve'

'They are all very good to Mother' is a quote from Eric Thomas' caption for the photograph of Gert and Cliff with a larger group on the verandah of the North Lyell Hotel—see Page 52.

p. 73: 'The mill'

Detail about Cliff Bradshaw buying Jim Morrison's sawmill and moving it up from the King River from the Tasmanian Special Timbers website—about us. (Accessed 1 July 2024) https://www.tasmanianspecialtimbers.com.au/about/

p. 75: 'Music and Pictures'

Italicised quotes are lyrics from It's a Long Way to Tipperary and Keep the Home Fires Burning—taken from 'Songs the Won the War' held in the Australian War Memorial sheet music collection, featuring verses from popular songs during World War I. Accession number AWM2016.30.44

p. 84: 'Gramophone'

Italicised quotes are lyrics from 'Between two trees' by Virginia Walsh and Ted Johnson. Sheet music held in the National Library of Australia—call no. MUS N mbb 783.242164 W227.

Matriarch

p. 93: 'Welcome'

Aspects of this description are based on the Western Wilds Story Stop 'We're alive to tell the story' a recording of Vicki Knowles (nee Bradshaw) by the Wayfarer Story Studio, Hobart on SoundCloud: https://soundcloud.com/thewayfinder/were-alive-to-tell-the-story?in=thewayfinder/sets/western-wilds-story-stops

p.94: 'Addition'

Text from newspaper clipping in the Bradshaw family collection headed 'King Billy Pine. The Phantom Forest', author Harry Frauca, publication unknown. Published online by ABC News on 23 October 2023: https://www.abc.net.au/news/rural/2023-10-27/king-billy-huon-sawmill-last-custodian-of-rare-tasmanian-timbers/103015506

p. 100: 'The tower'

Inspired by sheet of four photographs captioned 'THE STACK WAS DEMOLISHED 4-4-1975' displayed in the Galley Museum.

p. 107: 'The Knack'

Italicised quotes are lyrics from 'Between two trees' by Virginia Walsh and Ted Johnson. Sheet music held in the National Library of Australia—call no. MUS N mbb 783.242164 W227.

p.108: 'What Tasmania stands to lose'

Draws from information in "The King River and the Lairmerenga—what Tasmania Stands to Lose', Tasmanian Aboriginal Centre, 1991.

p. 116: 'King River Power Development as Triumphal Corporate Elegy'

Found text from voiceover narration written by Warren Hadfield for 1992 Hydro Electric Commission corporate video 'Long Live the King' commemorating commissioning of the King River Power Development. Published with permission from Hydro Tasmania. Full video can be viewed at: https://www.youtube.com/watch?v=9fYlOJh-4EE

Thereafter

p. 124: 'Care and Maintenance'

The facts in this poem were gathered from various ABC News articles about the accidents and the Coroner's Inquest, including: https://www.abc.net.au/news/2021-06-18/copper-mine-tasmania-deaths-avoidable-coroner-finds/100225168

p. 126: 'Crotty, 2016'

Details from Hobart Mercury article on 14 February 2016: https://www.themercury.com.au/news/tasmania/mining-ghost-town-on-tasmanias-west-coast-rises-from-depths-of-lake-burbury-in-summer-dry/news-story/

p.128: 'Bread'

Inspired by a banner hung on a Queenstown pub balcony during the 2018 Unconformity Festival.

p. 129: 'Reading list'

In compiling the list of Palawa writers (including poets, non-fiction and fiction writers, playwrights and artists who write), I was assisted by Melinda Susan Smith's 2020 PhD dissertation 'Trugernanner's Bones: Decolonization and Indigenous Futurity in Palawa Representations', accessed as a pdf via https://scholarspace.manoa.hawaii.edu/.

p. 130: 'Rings and ripples'

The family represented in this poem is not comprehensive. My apologies to anyone whose name I was not able to track down, as represented by ***. The family will, of course, continue to grow and change over time, and this page will become more and more out of date.

p. 131: 'Delta'

The details canvassed in this poem were drawn from articles and papers including: https://www.dcceew.gov.au/science-research/supervising-scientist/publications/ssr/remediation-options-tailings-deposits-king-river-and-macquarie-harbour and https://link.springer.com/article/10.1007/s10230-023-00943-5

p.134: 'Power'

The boxed quotes are from: https://tasmanian.com.au/powered/ and https://www.firstnationscleanenergy.org.au/tasmania_policy_overview_first_nations_and_clean_energy

Other statistics quoted come from:

https://www.premier.tas.gov.au/site_resources_2015/additional_releases/powered-by-tasmania-a-remarkable,-renewable-future

https://nre.tas.gov.au/Documents/Forestry%20Fact%20Sheet%202022-23.pdf

https://australiainstitute.org.au/post/native-forest-logging-in-tasmania-the-facts/

List of illustrations

These illustrations are monotype prints by the author, produced using photographs, botanical specimens from Queenstown and surrounds, and vintage crochet doilies. The sources of photographs and details of other material are described and listed below.

Cover	Photograph of Gert and Cliff supplied by Gay Bon, with celery top pine provided by Norman Bradshaw
p. 8	Moss
p. 10	Moss
p. 12	Moss
p. 14	Ferns
p. 18	Huon pine sample supplied by Norman Bradshaw
p. 23	Musk daisy bush
p. 24	Photograph of Crotty smelter from Queenstown Galley Museum
p. 28	Photograph of Mount Lyell Mine wood loaders from Queenstown Galley Museum, with huon pine sample supplied by Norman Bradshaw
p. 30	Lichen
p. 34	Photograph of Crotty, and title from map of Crotty, from collection of Queenstown Galley Museum
p. 36	Photograph supplied by Gay Bon, with vintage doily
p. 40	Photograph of Gert with brother supplied by Gay Bon. Map of Crotty from collection of Queenstown Galley Museum
p. 43	Myrtle
p. 44	Photograph of Gert with brothers from State Library of Tasmania collection, with fern
p. 47	Photograph of Gert supplied by Norman Bradshaw with celery top pine
p. 48	Photograph of Cliff Bradshaw and Ted Street supplied by Norman Bradshaw
p. 51	Wedding photograph of Gert and Cliff supplied by Ian Bradshaw, with vintage doily
p. 52	Photograph of group at North Lyell Hotel in collection of Queenstown Galley Museum with native laurel, and caption by Eric Thomas
p. 55	Photograph of Gert and Cliff supplied by Gay Bon. Map of Princess River lease from State Library of Tasmania collection
p. 57	Photograph of river monitoring station supplied by Norman Bradshaw, with map of Bradshaw lease in the collection of the State Library of Tasmania

p. 60	Photograph of Gert with children supplied by Gay Bon, with photograph of Princess River Mill from the Bradshaw family collection
p. 64	Map of Mount Lyell Open Cut mine, from the collection of the Queenstown Galley Museum, with myrtle
p. 66	Photograph of Gert with son supplied by Ian Bradshaw, with map of open cut from Galley Museum
p. 68	King Billy Pine sample supplied by Norman Bradshaw
p. 71	Photograph of Gert with brother Tom and other family members supplied by Ian Bradshaw, with fern
p. 72	Photograph of Cliff supplied by Gay Bon combined with author's photograph of sawn timber at Pioneer Traders, Lynchford
p. 76	Moss
p. 80	Photograph of Gert supplied by Gay Bon.
p. 82	Photograph of gymnastic troupe from the Queenstown Galley Museum, with moss.
p. 86	Photograph of Gert supplied by Gay Bon, with vintage doily.
p. 92	Photograph of Bren Gun carrier from Bradshaw family collection.
p. 95	Photograph of children from Bradshaw family collection.
p. 97	Photograph of house at Princess River from Bradshaw family collection.
p. 98	Photograph of Gert and Cliff supplied by Norman Bradshaw, with vintage doily.
p. 106	Photograph of Gert with family members supplied by Gay Bon, with vintage doily.
p. 110	Photograph of Gert and Cliff supplied by Ian Bradshaw with photograph of Bradshaw Bridge under construction supplied by Norman Bradshaw.
p. 113	Photograph of Crotty Dam supplied by Norman Bradshaw, with fern.
p. 114	Photograph from newspaper clipping in the Queenstown Galley Museum collection with map of Bradshaw lease from State Library of Tasmania collection.
p. 118	Photograph of Gert supplied by Norman Bradshaw, with vintage doily.
p. 123	Huon pine specimen supplied by Norman Bradshaw.
p. 127	Photograph of fire-ravaged King Billy pines at Joyce Creek from Bradshaw family collection with map of Bradshaw lease from State Library of Tasmania collection.
p. 133	Bearded heath
p. 138	Grass

About the Author

Jacqui Malins is a writer, performer and visual artist based on Ngunawal and Ngambri country in Canberra. She is fascinated by the dynamics and relationships of social and natural environments, and the patterns and forces shaping them over time. You can find her work on page, stage, in galleries and online: www.jacquimalinsart.com.

Jacqui has created poetry-theatre shows 'Matter of Life', 'Words in Flight' and 'Cavorting with Time' and performed at events including the Poetry on the Move and National Folk Festivals (ACT), the Woodford Festival (QLD) and the 2022 National Poetry Month Gala (NSW). She co-founded Mother Tongue Multilingual Poetry Events (Canberra), and directed and produced the 2021 and 2023 Poetic City Festivals.

www.ingramcontent.com/pod-product-compliance
Lightning Source LLC
Chambersburg PA
CBHW061119070526
44583CB00028B/3340